Something to Do

by Carol Talley

illustrated by Don Dyen

Editorial Offices: Glenview, Illinois • Parsippany, New Jersey • New York, New York
Sales Offices: Needham, Massachusetts • Duluth, Georgia • Glenview, Illinois
Coppell, Texas • Ontario, California • Mesa, Arizona

Every effort has been made to secure permission and provide appropriate credit for photographic material. The publisher deeply regrets any omission and pledges to correct errors called to its attention in subsequent editions.

Unless otherwise acknowledged, all photographs are the property of Scott Foresman, a division of Pearson Education.

Photo locators denoted as follows: Top (T), Center (C), Bottom (B), Left (L), Right (R), Background (Bkgd)

Illustrations: 3 – 19 Don Dyen; Photographs: 20 Digital Vision

ISBN: 0-328-13413-9

When I heard that Grandpa was coming to live with my dad and me in Willow Creek, I thought that it would never work. I know Grandpa pretty well, and I just couldn't picture him anyplace but in his old neighborhood in the city, with his old friends who lived on the block. But after Grandma died, Grandpa was positive that he couldn't get along all by himself. He said he was ready to move to the country and slow down.

Dad and I love Grandpa, and we did everything we could to make him feel at home at our place. We fixed up the best bedroom in the house just for him, with his old reclining lounge chair and a nice TV. We put his pictures of Grandma and our family on the dresser. I even put my aquarium in his room so he'd have some company during the day while I was at school and Dad was working at the Willow Creek Café. We wanted Grandpa to be comfortable.

Well, he was comfortable—too comfortable!

Every morning Dad left to open up the café, I left for school, and Grandpa settled into his old chair for a day of TV and snoozing. That's where we found him when we got home.

"Grandpa needs something to do," I said. "He needs to get some exercise."

Dad bought Grandpa a nice new pair of walking shoes and one of those pedometers you wear around your ankle that tells you how far you've gone. But Grandpa said that every time he went walking some big old dog came after him or he nearly got run over by a pickup truck.

"What's the sense in walking if you don't want to go anywhere?" said Grandpa. Grandpa sat in his lounge chair watching TV and the pedometer sat on his dresser.

"Maybe we could get Grandpa an exercise bicycle," I said. "We could set it right in front of the TV and he could peddle all afternoon right through the soap operas." Dad said we couldn't afford one of those right now.

"Well, he still needs something to do," I said. "Maybe a nice hobby he could do at home." So Dad bought Grandpa a pyrography set.

"What is it?" asked Grandpa. I had the same question.

Dad explained how you heated up the special tool and burned pictures or sayings onto wooden plaques. Well, this pyrography went over like a lead balloon. In other words, Grandpa didn't like it at all.

"I can't draw," he said. "Never could."

As for burning sayings into wood, Grandpa said he couldn't read his own writing even when he wrote with a regular ballpoint pen. Grandpa finished just one project, a sign that said, "DO NOT DISTURB! SLEEPING!"

About the only thing I could ever get Grandpa to do was to go with me down to the Willow Creek Café and hang out. I would help Dad a little, taking the trash out to the dumpster, sweeping the floor, folding napkins, stuff like that. Grandpa would read all the notices on the bulletin board—free kittens, houses for rent, backhoe services, and farm auctions. Then he'd settle into a corner table and watch the TV on the wall.

"That man needs something to do," said Trish, the waitress. "Maybe he needs a job."

"Yeah," I agreed.

Well, it turns out Trish was smarter than the rest of us. We might have never found that out, though, if Dad hadn't had those two pieces of pie left over one night at closing time.

"Here," Dad said to Grandpa and me. "Eat these or I'll have to throw them out." Dad settled down to go over his account books, and I dug right in.

"Not bad pie, huh, Grandpa?"

"I've had worse," said Grandpa, chewing a bite and staring up at the game show on the TV. "But I've had better too," he said, and now he was not looking at the TV, but just kind of staring off into space. "Remember those *fried* pies your Grandma used to make?"

"Oh, yeah," I said. "I could barely wait for them to cool off!"

"You're right, Dad," said Dad, looking up from his books. "Those fried pies were grand. They were heavenly!"

"Yes," said Grandpa. "Fried pie heaven. Grandma was rightfully prideful about those pies. What I wouldn't give for one right now!"

"Well," I said, "let's make some!"

"Us?" said Grandpa. "I don't know how to make fried pies. I only know how to eat them."

"But you must have watched Grandma make them a thousand times. Can't you remember how she did it?"

"Of course not," said Grandpa.

While we were talking, I was pulling Grandpa into the café kitchen. "Oh, come on," I said. "Think back. Didn't you pay any attention?"

"Well, I remember flour," he said. "She mixed up a bunch of flour."

"Mixed it with what?" I asked, opening up the flour bin and pulling a big bowl off the shelf.

Dad looked up from his books. "Flour and lard," he called. "Flour and lard and maybe a little salt. And you two better clean up that mess when you're finished!"

Grandpa found the can of lard and threw a couple big spoonfuls into the bowl with the flour. He added some salt, and I started stirring.

"Wait a minute," said Grandpa. "I don't think that's how she did it." He stared at the bowl for a minute and then he smiled. "Step aside, boy."

Grandpa stuck his big hands in the bowl and started squishing and mashing all that flour and lard with his fingers. "Yes," he said. "This is just how she did it! I remember now. Just squished it and squeezed it until . . . see! It's all getting blended together."

"It looks peculiar, Grandpa," I said. "It looks like little marbles! How's it supposed to stick together?"

Grandpa scratched his head, which wasn't such a good idea with all that flour and lard on his hands. "You're right," he said. "Something is missing." Grandpa wandered over to the shelves of jars and canisters along the wall. He shook his head. He usually recalls when he thinks about it, I figured. He went over to the big refrigerator, pulled the door open, and stared inside. Then his face lit up. "Here we go!" he said. "An egg is what we need. She added an egg!"

"Great!" I said. Grandpa cracked the egg into the bowl, and I stirred it into the mix.

The next step was the rolling pin, and by now Dad couldn't help but join in. Dad rolled the dough into a flat sheet. I opened up a can of peaches. Grandpa heated up the grease in a big black skillet. Then we got an assembly line going. Dad cut the dough into circles and put a big spoon of peaches on each one, I folded the circles in half and crimped the edges with a fork, and Grandpa slid the pies into the frying pan.

Well, I can't say those fried pies were perfect or as good as the ones Grandma used to make. Some of them had too much filling, and some didn't have enough. Some fell apart before they even got into the frying pan. Some didn't get cooked quite enough, and we burned some. But you know what? For the first time since Grandpa came to Willow Creek, it looked like he was really having fun. Even though the clock on the wall said it was way past Grandpa's usual bedtime, it looked to me like he was wide awake!

Remember what Trish said about Grandpa needing a job? Well, that's just where this fried pie episode went. Oh, sure, Grandpa had to improve his technique. He had to get his measurements down and improve his timing, but Dad and I finally convinced him that what the Willow Creek Café needed was a touch of fried pie heaven.

Now, most mornings Grandpa is up early and down at the café making fried pies. On the menu they're called Grandma's Fried Pies. It is kind of a memorial tribute to Grandpa's inspiration.

Lots of mornings I'm down at the café too, just helping out, selecting the flavor of the day—blueberry, apple, strawberry-rhubarb, or our favorite, peach! I make a few helpful suggestions like, "Hey! You didn't get enough filling in that one," "That one's a little lopsided," or, "If you don't get these pies out of the pan right now they are all going to be burnt to a crisp!"

But mainly I just watch Grandpa work his fried pie magic, glad that he's finally enjoying life in the country.

Families and Grandparents

Some kids have grandparents who live in other towns or even in other states. These kids can keep in touch with their grandparents with cards, letters, e-mail, and telephone calls. They can also enjoy their grandparents' company during visits.

Other kids visit their grandparents almost every day. Their grandparents might live nearby, or even in the same house. About six million grandparents in the United States live in the same home with their grandchildren. In some cases, kids live in the homes of their grandparents and are being raised by them.

Do you have a grandparent or special older person who you like to spend time with? Where does that person live? What do you like to do together?